A Box of Peppermints

A Box
of
Peppermints

by
Libby Stopple

Illustrated
by
Martha Bell

AMERICAN UNIVERSAL ARTFORMS CORPORATION

ISBN: 0-913632-07-4 Paper
ISBN: 0-913632-08-2 Cloth

Library of Congress Catalog Card Number: 75-20957

Printed in the United States of America

First printing   October 1975
Second printing   January 1976
Third printing   February 1981
Fourth printing   January 1985
Fifth printing   March 1989

A DROMGOOLE BOOK
Published by American Universal Artforms Corporation

Dedication

For
Julia, Walter and Patrick,
Frank and Lora, Joan and George
and Bill

Peppermints

No two are ever quite the same,
The candymakers say—
Yet who can tell the many moods,
Or where the mystery lay?

What moment in the melon seed,
Does Summertime begin;
How does the bird become the song —
And where have the Children been?

Contents

Preface

The world of the child is the world itself, for children are just little people upon this planet: little people perhaps even more poignantly aware of darkness and light, sorrow and gladness, than those older persons who surround them. The innocent joy and sadness a child feels, is as real as the universe in which he or she lives, and as big as the universe that lives within her or him. His purpose in life is the same as that of any human: to *grow in consciousness*; and he accepts it as naturally and spontaneously as he accepts his guilts and fears, his humor and high spirit. He or she simply *is*. They simply *are*.

I offer this Box of Peppermints to you, children of all ages; may you dip into its contents, as you would dip into your own memory — back to a time when you were already older than you knew, wiser than you thought. It is all here to stir your heart once again, just as it did yesterday . . . or was it the day before?

Libby Slappe

Dallas, Texas

Me

Aunt Ella
Gave me a box of Peppermints
The other day.

First thing I did
Was peep under the top layer,
To see if they were
All there.

Three things
I like best:
My old toy horse,
Peppermints,
And that music box
Granma's going to give me
Just as soon as she goes
To the Glory Land.

4

*O*nce
I kept my Sunday clothes on
All day long,
And no one came to
See us.

When the lady next door
Offered me a banana,
I took two —
One for my sister.
She doesn't like
Them.

I ran around the block
This morning —
First I tied that old cow bell
Around my neck.

It happened just like it did
Last time:
All the people came running
Out of their
Houses.

I guess the same man
Makes the pillows
That makes the
Marshmallows.

I don't think
I'll see-saw anymore
With that fat girl that wants
To play with me
At recess —

The way it ends up,
She does most of the seeing
And all I do is just
Sit there and
Saw.

*G*ranma
Had to write me a note last week,
For being so late
To school.

It was the June bug's fault.
I tied a long string around his stomach,
Only he kept turning around
And walking
The other
Way.

I

Stood on my head
This morning a long, long time.

When I got tired
I turned the world
Right side up
And went on in
And had my lunch.

I found
A tiny rock
Out in our alley
Yesterday.

It was shaped so like a heart
That I ran quick
And put it in my secret box.

The same box where I keep the red feather
That the robin
Gave me.

I was lying
On top of this hill
Looking at the sky
When all of a sudden
My arms started moving
And I floated up, up, up —
All the way up
To Kingdom Come.

Then I started down.
I came down fast
But it didn't hurt much.
The only thing was
I landed on my stomach
And that's how I got all this grass
In my mouth.

Aunt Ella asked me
If I could have something extra special
In the whole wide world,
What would it
Be?

All I could think of
Was could I hold a real live
Baby chicken
In my hand
Some
Day?

*M*y teacher
Called me a ring leader,
Once.

She said it wasn't just because
I could run the fastest
And talk the loudest
Either.

Grass,
Flowers,

& Getting Wet

15

We
Went to the store
This morning
After it stopped raining.

I walked
Right thru All the mud puddles
So's Granma
Wouldn't get her feet
Wet.

Papa
Says rain
Makes things grow.

I stood out in the rain
All morning
With my toes in the mud,
But Granma says I really
Didn't get any Bigger.
It's just that my pants
Shrunk.

*T*here was
This old frog
Out in our garden.
It started to rain
And he hopped
Under
A stone.

Next time it rained
I hopped under that same stone.
All of me got wet
Except my
Toes.

They
Let me water the lawn
Last night.

I held the nozzle straight up
And let the water come down
Like rain. . .
Because that's the way
The grass likes it
And I didn't
Mind.

*O*ne day
Last summer
When I didn't have anything else to do,
I climbed up to the top
Of an old hill.

I sat down next to a sunflower
And just wiggled my toe.
My big one.

*E*verything
Must be mixed up
Into one real *Big.*

I looked
Way deep inside a buttercup this morning,
And there was this little
Piece of sky.

*A*nd when
I stooped over
To pick that little violet
This morning,
It looked all fresh and happy
Like company was
Coming.

I'll go back
Tomorrow.

*T*here
Was this tiny crocus
In the grass.
It was standing on tip-toe
And pointing up
Like it was trying
To tell me
Something.

I put my head down low
To listen,
But I guess
My ears
Got
In
The
Way.

Papa

23

Papa says
To learn about things
You have to just
Dig in.

That's why I go barefooted
In the summer,
So's my toes can find out
About grass and mud
And stuff.

Papa says
There's a reason
For everything.

I guess
The reason we don't have to bathe
As much as cats,
Is 'cause we only have
Two elbows.

I asked
Papa a question.
He smiled and said
To let it be.

I wonder
If it was because the answer
Was too everywhere
And too spread out
Thin?

25

When Papa kissed me last night,
He looked all sad
Like when he's thinking
About Mama and how she went away
To be with God.

I kissed him back
Real extra
Hard.

I
Was going to ask Papa
A question
The other night,
When I saw this crack of light
Under the door.
I wondered if I made myself
All thin and flat
If I could slide under it —

Wouldn't that surprise everybody!

And then I forgot
What the question
Was.

Papa says
If I don't watch out
And slow down
I might end up in the next world.

This morning
I turned five somersaults in a row
Without stopping —
But when I opened my eyes
All I was doing
Was just sitting
Behind old Mr. Ben's
Barn.

Granma

27

*G*ranma
Didn't know
How pretty and peppermint
The world was,

Until I let her look thru
That old piece of pink glass
I found out in the alley
The other day.

Last night
I was about to climb our ladder.
The moon was on crooked
And I Explained to Granma
I wanted to straighten it —
Granma explained
No.

*S*ometimes
I sit under the table
And think about things
Like what if Each speck of dust
Is a whole wide world
With tiny people on it?
Wouldn't it be a shame
To wipe them
Away?

Then Granma comes in
And says to hurry
With my dusting.

I don't know why
Granma frowned so this morning
At the breakfast table.

That old dead chicken
I found yesterday
Did look like a church,
And all those little ants
Did look like the Saints
Come marching
In.

I guess
A little white lie
Is like when I don't tell Granma
That Santa Claus
Is just
Papa?

I helped
Decorate the tree
Last year,
And we kept running out
Of candy canes —

Granma says
I'll be in charge
Of the cardboard Angel
Next year.

I use to sprinkle powdered sugar
In the places where I licked the icing
Off the cake.

That was right before
Granma started putting cakes
On the top
Shelf.

Sometimes
Granma calls me
Her slow
Child.

That's when I climb
Up in her lap
And hug her real hard
So's she'll know how happy
And Hurry
I am.

*G*ranma
Wanted to know why
I was putting all that butter
In my hair
This morning —

That's when I told her
About how hard it is
To catch a greesed pig
And Charlie won't be pulling
My hair any
More.

Stars, Moon, Sun, Sky and a Mountain

Starting on a trip
In the wee dark hour of the morning
Is like everything loves you.

Even the moon doesn't want you to leave
And tags along
Over your shoulder.

I heard
Aunt Ella
Say it was high noon.
I ran quick outside
To see how high it was.

Everything
Was standing straight up
To the sun.
Even the shadows
Weren't lying down
Like usual.

*O*ne night I called everybody
To come quick and see
The moon.

It was sitting on top
Of our Chinaberry tree,
And it looked just like
That old white tea cup of ours —

The one with the handle off
And it doesn't have any
Saucer.

I climbed
Up in our old pecan tree
Last night,
And peeped between two leaves,
And there was this great big bright star!

I put the two leaves back together again,
And climbed down.
I haven't told anyone
About this.

A
Little star
Got caught in the tip
Of our elm tree, last night.
I wanted to climb up
And shake it loose
But Papa said to never mind:
It would be gone
By morning.

Only thing was
I wonder if it ever caught up
With the others?

Wonder
Why my heart beats so big
When the first star
Comes out?

*P*apa says
Sometimes a star falls.
I ran out in our back yard
And looked and looked.
All I could find special
Was three doodle bugs
And an old rusty
Spoon.

I sure do like
To do water-color pictures,
Only thing Is, my sky
Keeps running
Down
Into
My
Grass.

I saw this mountain:
It sure did look wrinkled and worried —
I guess that was because
It was holding this little lake
In its lap,
And didn't want
To spill any.

*L*ast summer
We visited a mountain.
I said:
Hello mountain.
Here I am.
This is me.

And the old mountain
Just sat
There.

*O*ne afternoon
I saw the moon
Still up in the sky —

I guess somebody
Just forgot
To turn
It
Off.

It gives me a sadness
To think about stars,
Shining, shining,
Always shining
And never ever
Getting
Shined
On.

Sister
&
My Brother

43

We
Had this old, white cat,
And my sister painted his whiskers green,
To match his eyes —
I liked him better the way he was
Before he ran off to the woods
And didn't come
Back.

Sometimes
My sister just looks at me,
At the table —

Then Granma says
For us to fold our napkins
And go somewhere else
To giggle.

*M*y sister
Used to walk up and down the room,
With a book on her head.
She said it would make her
More graceful.

Now I wonder
Do *all* graceful people
Have flat
Heads?

I
Guess my sister
Didn't know Granma
Was standing right behind her
When she said how someday
She'd tell Granma
A thing
Or two.

*M*y brother
Jumped off the barn last week:
He was holding on to Granma's
Old, black umbrella—

That one there,
The one that leans sideways
And is turned
All inside
Out.

Birds & Squirrels

...and the other Cat

Sometimes
That old, speckled hen of ours,
Turns her head sideways
And holds it
Close to the ground.
Close to the ground.
Papa says she's listening
For worms.

I don't see how she can tell
Which is the talking end though,
Do you?

I'd sure
Like to be a bird.

Only thing is,
Wonder why they
Eat
Worms?

We
Went to the beach once,
And I heard this sea gull crying
As it flew out
Over all that
Water —

I guess it was already
Homesick.

49

*N*ext
To being me,
I'd like to be
A big, black bird,
Then I could sit up in my tree
All day long,
And think
And think
And think
About nothing
But
Bird
Things.

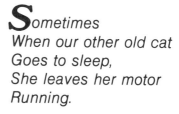

*S*ometimes
When our other old cat
Goes to sleep,
She leaves her motor
Running.

My sister said
If I'd look into her ears,
Maybe I could See it,
But I never
Have.

I guess she keeps it
Somewhere
Else.

*P*apa says
The squirrels
Chase off the birds. . .
But I guess they make up
At bedtime,

'Cause everything is quiet
Until next morning
When the birds come back all fresh
And ready to be chased
Off again.

Other People

I was taking
Those empty pop bottles
Back to the store,
When I saw
This

rich dog.

He was sitting there
In the back seat
Of this shiny, black car.
I didn't say anything
To him
Either.

*A*unt Ella
Tells the best
Bedtime stories.

I always like the part
That comes right after
The *and so thens.*

*P*apa says there must be an Angel
On my shoulder.

I wish he'd tell Aunt Ella
About this;
She's always hitting me
On the back
To make me stand
Up straight.

Charlie and I
Pushed thru the jungle
Out in our back yard:
We knew when we got to Africa,
'Cause it was dark
And we saw a native.

He was just getting ready
To shrink our heads
When his mother
Called him in
To do his
Home work.

*W*e went to the zoo.
I was standing watching the lions,
When this man came by and said
Lions ate people.

I asked him
If it was the same
As like when people
Ate cows?

He
Just
Walked away.

*I*t was right after
Papa said how some people
Never know when to keep their mouths
Shut,
That I saw this man
Standing on the corner.

I told him how
He could close his mouth
Any time he wanted to.
Last time I looked back
It was still
Open.

*M*r. Ben says
Time goes by so fast —

I guess it sure is in a big hurry
To get where it's headed for,
'Cause it's always gone
When I get
There.

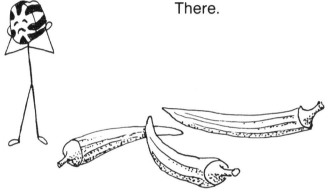

*S*omeday
I'm going out
And try to find that child
That lives *somewhere.*

You know:
The one Papa's always telling me about,
Who doesn't have any Sunday shoes,
And would be *glad* to *have*
That piece of okra
I left on my
Plate?

*T*here's
That old skinny man
Down the street,
That never
Smiles.

I guess his mouth
Doesn't know about
How to
Up.

The people down the street,
Have this old bull dog,
And he just sits and sits
By the front gate.

Granma says
They had a little boy once, too,
Only he went away to war
And didn't come
Back.

Bugs and Frogs, Spiders and Turtles, Puppies and Mice

...and a Lizard

I
Guess cock roaches just *are* —
They can't help
It.

*H*is little face was so sweet
And his paws were all folded over.
Granma shook him from the trap
And said he must
Have come in
From outside.

I had to ask God
Would He please go out
And tell the others
Not to come in,
'Cause I don't talk
Any *mouse*.

*W*e played church today.
I was the preacher.
I told about Noah
And how he built that big boat
Right before the river flooded.

Then I told
How he chased two of everything
Inside —
Even two grand-daddy-long-legses.

*N*ow I never have seen
A dead butterfly. . .

I guess they just don't
Stay in one place
Long enough
To.

*I*t was getting late
And there was this little brown bug,
Trying to get from one leaf
To another —
I put a blade of grass
Across,
But he went all the way
Around.

I guess he didn't know
What time
It was.

My little turtle
Died last week,
And Aunt Ella gave me her jewel case
To bury him in.

This morning I dug him up
To see if he was resting in peace,
He was.

We're
All busy, today:
Granma and Aunt Ella
Are putting up preserves,
Papa's cleaning the barn,
And if I ever have another
Little turtle,
I'm going to teach him
To talk.

*O*nce
My brother dared me
To wear his pet lizard to school
On my shoulder—

How did I know
It was going to wake up
And I'd have to go and give it
To the Principal?

I built
A little rock wall
Around that poor, old frog
Out in our garden,
So's I could go out and talk
With him sometimes. . .
And keep him company.

Anyway
He hopped over the wall—
I guess he didn't know
How lonesome
He was.

I
Like to hear
The crickets in the night.
It's like everything
Has come home.

*T*he other day
I was all bent over,
Talking to that doodle-bug hole,
When Charlie came by and wanted to know
What I was
Doing.

I saw
This grasshopper
This morning.
He had his elbows
Propped on his knees.

I guess he was tired.
His hopper was turned off
Too.

*T*here was this little puppy.
He buried something
In our back yard.
When he was asleep
I tip-toed over
And dug it
Up.

It was just an old piece
Of watermelon rind.
Wonder why do puppies always sleep
With one eye
Open?

*B*ees are funny
Aren't they?

I guess they're just so busy
Inventing honey
And stuff.

I built
This tiny house of sand
Right on the edge of bedtime.
Then early next morning
I ran out to see if it was still there,
And I found these tiny tracks.

Wonder where they're headed for. . .
All these little bug folks
Who walk around barefoot
In the night?

66

God
and
Old Men

*T*here
Was this old man
With the white hair and beard.
He was leaning down his cane,
And he looked like
He'd come
A long
Way —

Wonder
Was he
God?

Granma says
Old folks and children
Are closer to God
Than anyone.

Wonder
If that's who
That old lady out in her back yard,
Was talking to the other day,
When there was no one around but me. . .
And I was hiding?

Last night
I looked out the window
And said my prayers
Through the big bare branches
Of our apple tree.

This morning
My heart feels all Round inside,
Like a robin's
Breast.

An
Old man I know
Sits in his rocker and tells me
Stories
About covered wagons
And Indians
And all. . . .

Sometimes
He doesn't say anything —
He just sits and rocks
All the way back
To the day
When.

Me Again

73

I saw myself once,
In a mud-puddle
In the back yard. . .

I scooped me up;
But I spilled most of me
Before I could get inside
To show anybody.

*S*ummer
Is when the sun
Gets all lazy
And slows
Down.

Sometimes
It stays in one place so long
I have to just sit
Under a tree
And wait.

*S*ometimes
The wind
Gets in such a hurry,
It stumbles and bumps me
All the way down the block
Past my bedtime.

Sometimes
I wake up in the night
And think about
Little white ponies
With golden bells. . .

Then everybody comes in
And wants to know why
I'm clapping
My hands.

I had a whole
Pocket full of peppermints,
When that new girl from down the block,
Came by to play —

Wonder why you always
Have to be so nice
To people
You don't
Know?

Wonder
Why peppermints always taste
So squeaky-pink
And white?

A stomach ache
Is like when somebody
Gives you a box of candy
And by the time you remember
To be polite and pass it around,
It's all gone.

*E*verybody says
Mama was so pretty
People turned around
Just to look
At her.

Anyway. . .
The only reason that old Lady
Turned around yesterday,
Was 'cause I had
My dress on
Backwards.

I guess
I should have thanked the Lady
For the cookie, this morning,
But everybody's always saying
How you shouldn't talk
With your mouth
Full.

I had the merry-go-round
All to myself
This morning
In the
Park.

I took that old stick
With me —
The one with
The sharp
End.

Sometimes I just sit
On this bottom step
And wonder.

I wonder what there would have been
In the very beginsment
If there hadn't *been*
Any beginsment?

There's
A place I like to go
Only you don't get there
By walking anywhere special.
You just kinda disappear
Inside yourself.

Sometimes
Teacher taps real loud
On her desk,
And I have to come out so fast
I can hardly
Breathe.

I was walking
Thru this sunburnt meadow,
When I came upon a bush
Where a yellow bird
Had been —

It made me feel
So glad. . .so glad,
I ran
All the way down
The afternoon.

*S*ometimes
I climb up in that old tree
On the vacant lot. . .
The one that has the long limb
That rocks when the wind
Blows.

That way I can curl up
All by myself
And know I'm
Still
Me.

This is
A DROMGOOLE BOOK

by

AMERICAN UNIVERSAL ARTFORMS CORPORATION
Austin   Texas

DESIGNED
&
ILLUSTRATED
by
MARTHA BELL

ABOUT THE AUTHOR
and
ABOUT THE BOOK

Libby Stopple is internationally known as a lyric poet. She is also a wide-ranging composer of folk and art songs. Ms. Stopple is a former nurse—Charles A. LeMaistre, M.D., now Chancellor of the University of Texas, says: "Libby Stopple gives to her readers or to her patients *peppermints* every time she touches their lives. A truly remarkable person whose talents have made our world a better and brighter place."

Elected to the Poetry Society of America in 1955, she is a member and former officer of the Poetry Society of Texas, and honorary member of the Old Saturday Club of London, England. Her work has appeared in numerous anthologies in the United States and other countries; her awards and honors span this country, Italy, and Switzerland. Bishop Oxnam read her "Creed for the Universal Man" at the General Assembly of the United Nations. Her long poem, "Death of a Morning," was included in the Tenth Anniversary Service for John F. Kennedy, at the Memorial site in Dallas, November 21, 1973.

Leonora Speyer has said: "I find Libby Stopple's work moving, sincere. I like its simplicity."

Arthur Sampley: "Libby Stopple writes of the old verities with freshness and vitality."

Grace Noll Crowell once said: "God has been very sure of Libby Stopple. He has trusted her with joy and sorrow, peace and pain."

In Dallas schools and while Ms. Stopple was poet-in-residence in Corpus Christi, Texas, elementary schools in 1975, the contents of this book were exposed to some real live kids.

Bob Lasher wrote: "I LIKED YOUR BOOK ABOUT PEPPERMINTS. ESPESHELY THE ONE ABOUT THE GIRL AND THE MOUNTAIN."

Michelle Mason: "I LIKED THE ONE WHERE THE GIRL KLIMED THE LADDER TO FIX THE MOON."

David Hamer: "THE BEST ONE I LIKED IS WHEN HE BURRIES THE TURTLE."

Kathy Duval: ". . . BUT THE BEST ONE WAS WHEN THE GIRL PAINTED THE CAT GREEN TO MATCH HIS EYES."

We like the ones about the "rich dog," and the pecan tree, and not talking any "Mouse," and those about God and old folks.

Which will be yours?

The Publisher